To Skip,

I really enjoyed talking to you today! I hope you will enjoy this...

Echo (A.K.A Joe)

Joseph M Brennan

A Farewell to Reason

A Farewell to Reason

by Echo

Painted Petals
Press

First Printing, 1998

All artwork was created using International Microcomputer Software Inc. (IMSI) Master Clips, Corel Draw, and may include clip art from one or more of the following sources:

1) 3G Graphics

2) Archive Arts

3) BBL Typographic

4) Cartesia Software

5) Image Club Graphics Inc.

6) Management Graphics Ltd.

7) One Mile Up Inc.

8) Studio Piazza Xilo M.C.

9) Techpool Studios Inc.

10) Totem Graphics Inc.

11) TNT Designs

Library of Congress Catalog Card Number: 97-69737

ISBN: 1-891433-00-8

ATTENTION COLLEGES, UNIVERSITIES, AND CORPORATIONS: Quantity discounts are available on this book. For information contact the distributor at: 1-800-247-6553, web site: http://www.bookmasters.com. When calling, please provide the following information:

1) Name of Book -- A Farewell to Reason
2) Author -- Echo
3) Publisher -- Painted Petals Press

Acknowledgments/Dedication

This work was inspired by those that have touched my existence in ways they will probably never realize. These include my friends, my family, my co-workers, my fellow poets, my fans, and even a few strangers who have crossed my path. I thank them all for the wonderful journey they've given me so far. Their inspiration is written on the pages that follow. They will ever serve to inspire me.

Table Of Contents

Foreword

This book expresses the experiences and observations of a single man. Some of the writings contained reflect personal experiences, and others reflect experiences shared by those that have inspired me. It is my hope these writings will encourage readers to seek the inspirational fountains that surround their own lives, and enable them to discover the value of personal reflection. Through these means we can achieve a balance, filling our lives with greater joy and less regret.

May the pages that follow recall your own personal, emotional experiences. Only through the constant reawakening of these emotions can we reach a greater awareness of our selves, thus leading our lives down the path of greater purpose.

To those unafraid
to partake of
the drink of intrigue:

May you relate
to the pages
that follow . . .

Inside every man
there lies a poet
who died young
                    -- Stefan Kanfer

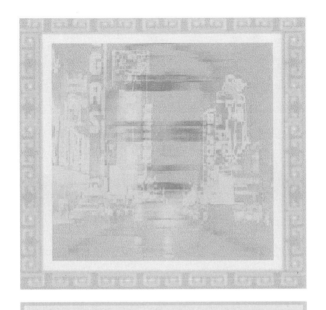

I. The Dressing Room

The Dressing Room

How many times we like to try on the T.V. screens, the Hollywood scenes filled with the gloss and glamour we can never own. Still it seems these Snow White illusions become the windows of our homes:

"Lights, Camera, Action": Boy meets girl; boy loses girl; boy travels around the world to win back girl . . .

"Lights, Camera, Action": Girl leaves boy for another boy; girl gets fancy treasures; girl gets nights filled with passion and pleasure . . .

"Lights, Camera, Action": Boy cheats on girl; becomes a model for Playgirl; on fame, everything he blames; writes somber words in letter back to girl . . .

Yes, it seems we all want just a little more. Over and again we sacrifice the hearts, the souls of the ones we love the most for no matter how many times we cheat, we lie: diamond stones always have a warm and welcome glow.

Night Dances

Can you see me,
a silhouette in a crowd,
for you walked into the room
and the room disappeared;

You move in soothing waves,
and there is little control
as I swirl into the warming haze
of alcohol and cigarette smoke;

You wrap me . . .   You wrap me . . .
into your spider's web
with seductive graces,
and nothing's sure for long;

A newspaper ring
is your commitment
when the dance is over,
but you visit often:

You tug at the blinds
in the back room,
late at night
when I'm home alone,
drawing me to feed
upon the images of bliss
you freely give
at your cabaret show,
-- images rented,
            but never owned.

Lisa Lingers

I see Lisa sometimes,
staring from behind
the window blinds
that line the raceways
of my runaway mind;
Love warms this rented room,
rapture smiles upon my eyes,
the thought of her just enough
to fill my want with wine;

I feel Lisa sometimes,
the fireplace glows
when her hands touch mine,
whispers breathe intrigue, I know
it was many hours ago;
Love warms this rented room,
rapture smiles upon my eyes,
the thought of her just enough
to fill my want with wine;

I cry for Lisa sometimes,
such color her passion paints;
Should I be surprised to find
my rainbows awash with rain?
Love warms this rented room,
rapture smiles upon my eyes,
the thought of her just enough
to fill my want with wine;

She stares from behind
the window blinds,
the fireplace glows
when her hands touch mine,
the color of her passion paints
my rainbows awash with rain,
. . . she fills my want . . .
. . . she fills my want . . .
and lingers whenever I awake.

The Firewalk

Our bodies sweat as we enter
the dark room downstairs,
-- the room with the dance beat,
the haunting dance beat;
I am helpless
as the melody threads
and passes through me
on the ends of knitting needles;

You lead the tribal ritual
as flames pour into
the middle of the room,
-- the battlefield proving ground;
It is time for the fire walk:
How much do I love you?
Bunker walls explode
when simple words ring true;

Tossed and tumbled
upon the air waves,
I careen into a spin
until I lose myself again;
I drift, I fade . . .
        I drift, I fade . . .
into the night
which cuts and ducks
deep into intrigue;

My head is but a whirlwind,
and it is difficult to discern
which images to save
and which to burn,
but as night dances begin to fade,
the persistent light of a new day
stands behind the window shades
to reveal what is lost and what remains.

Plastic Rose Petals

Glamour, fame, fashion, fortune!
Limousines, travel scenes, flashy interviews!
New York adores New York,
everything glimmers in New York!

Beauti-color faces such lasting treasure!
Flourescence always brings great pleasure!
Camera flashes -- take one, take two!
Mademoiselle, Vogue, Bizarre, GQ!

Talk show hosts and celebrity queens!
Glossy scenes polish television screens!
A dance of fantasies eager to please,
sell wonderland dreams as reality!

Domestic gloom presented in neon costume!
Hollywood stage lights -- the passion room!
We surround our lives with such gay cartoons,
and stand jury to these wallpaper truths.

Dream Infatuation

I want to reach you,
but I cannot escape the pain
or the shame I feel inside;

Yearning and conscience
struggle to dominate a splintered soul,
you're only inches from my fingertips,
and you may never know;

So I put you into a dream
where yearning and conscience
smear into a watercolor gray,
where numbness explodes
into images (passion) . . .
into images (desire) . . .

But images never leave,
they remain long after the dream is over
They taunt . . .
They tease . . .
They breathe . . .
(and i want to reach you)

So I put you into a dream,
only inches from my fingertips;
I put you into a dream,
and no one ever has to know.

Night Whispers

Night whispers
are the tender echoes
of distant sea gulls
fading into the sea;

Eyes meet eyes,
and a soothing bliss
overwhelms entire existence,
spinning perception and reason
helplessly beneath the undertow;

Awash on the waterfalls of time,
will a heart crash upon the rocks,
or glide upon slow, foaming fountains?

It matters not,
for only glossy images decide
when eyes meet eyes;

Night whispers unspoken
whip like the wind
upon a raging sea,
leaving all masts broken.

The Glance

I hold you hostage
within my eyes,
the vampire smile
feels right tonight,
for it will only be
a little while
before you'll
feel the need
to be with me;
Take a chance
on this passing glance,
or forever seek
this dream of intrigue;
The clandestine, dark,
and deep limousine
is waiting here
for you to leave;
Just the hint
of a quiet nod,
and we could soon
both be gone:

Where would you like to go
(the destination I have in mind
can portray any place you might know)?

What would you like to do
(the seeds of desire can bloom
from any root that you might choose)?

Give me a letter,
but let me guess the word,
this maze of puzzles build
the walls of this world;

Can you stand the waves
of your own curiosity,
play the starring role
within my midnight mystery?
Then say good-bye to all realities
for they won't live here tonight,
I exorcised these demons
long before you arrived;
So let yourself go . . .
                just let yourself go . . .
tumble all along the rows
of colliding, emotional dominos;
Bathe in the secrets
of the final, pleasant dream
for:
. . . you may never see . . .
. . . you may never feel . . .
. . . you may never breathe . . .
this way again;

Tell me not of the future,
tell me not of the past
for the eyes of dawn
will awaken soon,
and then is when
fresh virgins like you
begin to learn
to lose the truth.

The Snapshot

Tonight I am warmly
asleep with the sin,
though others might find
where I have been;
A night of pleasure
always precedes such pain,
but several hours still remain
before the midnight guards
march in the armies of the day;
Move me into the passion room
where roller coasters cascade
down the endless halls
of revolving walls;
Let the burning wheels
of mystery and intrigue
eternally flash and flame;
Let the stadium r-o-a-r!
Let the stadium r-o-a-r!
For nothing sacred is safe,
and nothing can be sure
when our breathless
whispers begin to:
. . . merge and blur . . .
. . . merge and blur . . .
. . . merge and blur . . .
. . . merge and blur . . .
. . . merge and blur . . .

Tell me more . . .
Yes, tell me more . . .
for I have never heard
these words before;

Come daybreak
only ashes remain
when we embrace
the morning masquerade;
-- a token wave
to the one
who drives away,
but no one
ever escapes
the taunting gaze
of the fireplace
that still remains.

Dark Waters Shallow . . .
Dark Waters Deep

She enters through the turnstiles,
-- a junkie to the wild and winding ride
that only a stranger's touch can give;
She knows not what she'll find,
but she wants to live a lifetime tonight;
In the shadows of a disco room
she wades . . .
within eyes of mystery;
Dark waters shallow,
yield to dark waters deep,
still she continues the journey,
for what lied around the corner
Pandora had to know,
-- she just had to know;

She surrenders to his power,
she surrenders to his prose
not knowing where this might go;
Hands explore elegance;
Hands explore stone;
After "final, last call" he decides
he wants to take her home;

A single night could be too much,
-- a million nights not enough;
He was the best she ever had
-- the best she ever had;

The night swallows
everything she owns
when her heartbeat
begins to lose control;
Does she scream in ecstasy . . .
Does she scream in pain . . .
in between the breathless pants
when he finally decided
she'd be better off dead,
-- she'd be better off dead.

II. The Passion Room

The Passion Room

Love is a cloud carefree upon the breeze -- ever tossed and turned, but knows not where it's going. It seems we ever search for the distant, summer shores where love is born, places where:

-- Smiles greet smiles by candlelight

-- Eyes sip champagne on faraway planes

-- Lips wrestle with breathless lips

In later days we find our hearts, once wild with rapture and rave, fall upon the velvet gray of quiet, September rain when we think of all the restless shores where we once played, but may never see again.

Moonlight Bay

Moonlight Bay bathes me
in silent serenity;
Gentle whispers of the cool breeze
soothe my tender thoughts;

Never before has it revealed itself
in such stunning brilliance:
Crystal waves shimmer beneath
showering, starlight fountains;

--The eyes of an angel, si
it was only the thought i n
g
and my spirits were . . . r

si n
i g
r
f
a
l g
$l_i n$
f
a
l g
$l_i n$ restless upon
the rushing surf;

The image breathes in memory
. . . t-a-u-n-t-i-n-g . . .
. . . t-e-a-s-i-n-g . . .
and although I reach
to capture every passing wave,
I cannot wash Moonlight Bay away.

Dawn of a Daydream

Spring over Crystal Lake
brought with her
a fresh bouquet of rose petals,
and butterflies in bloom;
She swam out of the ripples
of the sunrise reflection
to place another's kiss
upon my lips;
Images of new romance
massage into memory:
. . . tender face . . .
. . . tender touch . . .
. . . tender breath . . .
She wanders inconspicuously
into my noonday world
to secretly slip me away
from the staccato echoes
of computer keys;
Every day I pray
to never find
the sunset fading
from my lover's eyes,
for she is the one
who smiles the light
between the shadows
of an overcast day;
She is warm within my thoughts
through the long, long work day,
and she'll be warm within my heart
when I return home to her special place.

Carnation Serenade

Carnations yellow . . .
Carnations white . . .
whisper waveless words
that breathe by her bedside;
Serenade her soul
with my song tonight,
play any symphony
that gives her light;
Open windows
within her dreams,
give her peace
when she thinks of me;
Bring melodic moons,
intriguing perfumes,
breezy, seaside afternoons;
You carry the swan song
within my heart tonight,
please make her mine,
make her mine this time,
carnations yellow . . .
carnations white.

A Woman's Tease . . .
A Woman's Torture

It was the sweetest tease
I've ever known;
The most brutal torture
I've ever been shown:
-- The subtle scent
of a woman's perfume
barely out of reach;
-- The pale breath
of a lover's, lost heartbeat
sailing by setting sea;
I saw the look in her eyes
long before words
ever touched her lips,
felt her warmth
long before my face
brushed against her fingertips;
On restless, wanderlust nights
I galloped across the stormy seas
searching for pleasure within reach;
I was convinced that her torture
could not bring much more
till I awoke with the sense
that a kiss had passed,
but could not be sure,
-- the mid-morning dream
had raced away
at ultrasonic speed.

A Wedding in Fall

Gentle, the waltz to faraway places
lighting the candles along the way,
nourished by the breath of the sea,
caressed by music box melodies;
Nights fall upon days,
serene footsteps fade
to the intimate whispers
of rose petal raindrops;
Daybreak dances across
the waves of a warm embrace,
polishing the golden dawn
of love's eternal song;
Hearts weave between
the melodic moons,
and the wondrous hues
of a watercolor waltz for two;
Autumn leaves
descend into soft spiral,
the wind upon the waters wane,
but never the tender trace
of the kiss on this wedding day.

The Starring Role

I like the way
she looks at me
from across the bar
of blues melodies;
She reaches deep
between the forest trees
to find the lost,
little boy in me;
For just a moment
I warm her eyes
with his tender, shy,
little boy smile;
Champagne bubbles
suddenly surge inside
as nervous fingers try
to drum away my stage fright;
"Yes, I believe
I'll have another drink",
I like the way
she looks at me.

Want

The clouds that storm
along the midnight shore
make me want you even more;
I thirst for the rain,
-- the rain that never stops,
but you only feed
drop by single, narcotic drop;
--- Run away ---
I really believe I should,
but the Chinese, water torture
never felt so good,
and I ponder
how much longer
I can restrain the flood gates,
how much longer
I can contain the wait
before releasing the hands
that long to waterfall . . .
You finger-paint
across my windshield,
smearing the lanes
I thought were sure;
The freeway whirls
into a blur
as the arrogant, little,
sports convertible,
once firm upon the curve,
begins to:
. . . *spin out of control* . . .
. . . *spin out of control* . . .
. . . *spin out of control* . . .
. . . *spin out of control* . . .
. . . *spin out of control* . . .

You leave me lost . . .
You leave me lost . . .
in between things
you might have said,
and the things
I thought instead.

III. The Melancholy Room

The Melancholy Room

B e a u t i f u l . . . Why do you look more b e a u t i f u l . . . between the smoke rings, behind the tinted haze of drunken Saturdays, on hangover, Sunday afternoons when I wake to find I cannot remember the name of the girl leftover from the night before. Still I do not call, and the neglect only sinks me deeper into the mud of my own conscience. So I drink another beer as I watch summer embers glimmer upon the autumn leaves of long, lost loves. I dance with each of their shadows throughout the day, and ponder the number of yesterday's treasures tarnished by the things done today. Sometimes I wish I could find the boy in me, and melt the frost upon my beating heart. The wandering fields once so exciting in bloom, now fill with images of me and you, and the things we used to . . .

Ghost Channels

"Good-bye" in a crowded room,
I rehearse the word to myself,
across the current I look at you,
and cannot express the mood;
You extended your hand towards mine,
but the bank I could not reach,
  -- ghost channels wide,
        -- ghost channels deep;
Often within tomorrow's world
I dreamed with you I'd be,
although my eyes fill with sorrow,
I didn't ask you to wait for me;
"Good-bye" I see the somber wave
within your eyes as you turn to leave,
it seems I've waited in silence too long,
fresh, rose petals stale upon my lawn;
I hope you'll find that better place
where summers never fade,
I hope good things you someday find
won't dim my smile within your mind;
The words I spoke before were true
within your room of margarita moons;
I never meant you any harm,
sometimes I find I'm only wrong.

The Darkroom

The piano plays in the key of melancholy,
the sun begins to fade behind the blinds,
and she knows that it is time
to visit the empty room upstairs;

A pale smile touches her lips
as fingers brush across the smiling faces;
Frames chronological from boy to man
in the empty room upstairs;

In a myriad of scattered images,
tears of joy wed tears of pain,
and there is no one left to blame
in the empty room upstairs;

She holds his ghost in her arms,
rocks back and forth stroking his hair;
She knits memories in her waiting room
in the empty room upstairs;

Nothing moved in the passing years
except the dust on Wednesdays and Saturdays,
she hesitates, and then slowly turns away
from the empty room upstairs;

Another just like it across the hall,
photographs bedside: yellow, black, white;
-- the smiling couple on a glorious day,
. . . somber footsteps enter softly . . .
. . . somber footsteps enter softly . . .
the other empty room upstairs.

The Separation

Little girl . . . my little girl,
what will become of you,
the blooming petals of your fragile life
affected by the things adults do;

Will your virgin smile
wilt from the pain?
Will I ever be the one
to bow his head in shame?
For I will always feel
I was the one to blame;

Little girl . . . my little girl,
consequences transparent to you,
but I see the impact so clearly
driven by the things adults do;

Your kiss so sweet and innocent,
I hold you as if it were any other day,
but I hide such fear inside,
far away from your gentle eyes,
for the battle rages every night,
and no truce is ever signed;

If life could only be so simple
as coloring books and crayons,
the boundaries not so fickle,
and the color not so critical,
but guns pound through the night
reducing to rubble all that was once mine;

Little girl . . . my little girl,
will you recall how much I loved you,
for daddy's going away today,
-- a consequence of things adults do.

Porcelain, Painted as Stone

The porcelain statue
painted as stone,
falls outside
my second story window;

End over end it tumbles
in the space between,
helplessly awaiting
the final scene;

So many things
now clearly seen,
so many things
rush back to me;

A sunset falls upon my heart today
as you slowly drift away in time,
and I can only watch you fade,
a mother's eyes on a dying child;

My statue aimlessly tumbles,
and in the space between
only memories as I wait to sweep
away the shattered pieces;

For as you turn to leave
how could you know,
my porcelain was only
painted as stone?

Sand Crystals

A new crystal
to polish and place
into an endless chain,
-- an endless chain of memories;

How long I've waited
for just the opportunity
to increase the glimmer,
or the karat of the stone?

How long we've waited
for just the right moment,
the words to seal our fate,
investing in tomorrow lands?

Yesterday, eyes danced
in a celestial world
as we held each other close
in our candlelight ballet,
but the night is over,
the candles have melted;
I awoke today and polished
lost diamonds of the past.

Unprecedented Desire

Once while stranded at sea
I gripped the seething lifeline
tossed for someone else and not me,
your heart is where I yearned to be,
-- a photograph reminds me . . .

I'll never forget the way
you looked in those days,
colors that led me astray
were the colors that ever remained,
-- a photograph reminds me . . .

You were monumental when
my universe was small,
so little else back then
have I recalled,
-- a photograph reminds me . . .

Now nothing remains inside but "try",
and someday should my plane decide
to spin away from the sunset sky,
would you forever let me keep
the smooth, sentimental dream,
desire is not a passing thing,
-- a photograph reminds me . . .

Winding Country Road

Winding through the meadow lands,
through the forest lands too,
the rocky mountain crests
within your eyes so blue,
I shoveled through
the mud and clay,
laid the asphalt
that someday would fade,
for the road I paved
led far from here,
-- the road I built
for years and years;

Your misty silhouette
warms and kisses me
within the purple clouds
that sail melancholy seas,
but yesterday breathes not a sound,
and the only comfort I can find
is within the rhythm of the rain,
which drones away the echoes
along the road that still remains;

I hold you in a thousand ways,
touch the warmth of your face,
share unspoken words in time,
but the fog, the wind, the rain
is all you've left behind,
and the past is ever haunted
by the pages empty within my mind;
The trees guarding this country road
know exactly how I feel,
limbs stir within the island breeze,
but from here will never leave.

IV. The Room of Illusion

The Room of Illusion

Spring images paint the butterflies upon my eyes as words sing exotic melodies with relative ease, but deep inside hides the raging battlefield which never seems to sleep. The armies of logic and reason attack the armies of creativity, and they ever spin inside my mind . . . inside my mind . . . for no truce is ever signed:

When I find my paradise, there can be no disguise. Music cascades . . . This medal is presented to the family of corporal Weiss for his exceptional performance in the great war . . . *in dimensions four, five, six, nine as eyes fall upon the tie dye sky . . .* Corporal Weiss single handedly attacked a machine gun emplacement . . . [The force of attraction or repulsion between two point charges is directly . . . *The fields move into green into blue, into all other colors in between . . .* while under enemy fire, risking his own life for the lives of his peers and subordinates alike. This attack was critical to the success . . . proportional to the product of the individual point charges . . . And God Said: The people of Israel are my sheep, and I solemnly promise that they will live in peace. I will chase away every wild . . . *When I look back on all the places I might have been, I feel I must have lived . . .* of the invasion. The medal earned for this achievement is a symbol of courage and honor, and has only been awarded to a select group of military . . . and inversely proportional to the square of the distance between them] . . . animal from the desert and the forest, so my sheep will not be afraid. They will live around my holy mountain and I will bless them . . . --{ I think she might be looking at me, I wonder if she'll still be there after my girl friend leaves . . . }-- *in a dream for blue sometimes looked like red, and it seems I can only have been here or there instead . . .* leaders. Corporal Weiss has set a wonderful example for other military leaders to follow. He will be greatly missed by his peers, subordinates, and superiors alike.

Arrogance in Return

Brother can you tell me . . .
what is the color of my wall,
is it Spring or is it Fall,
for so many things I cannot recall
when bets are large and the gains small;

Brother can you tell me . . .
is there a humbler road that I can take,
so difficult to escape
when the past stands in my way,
and the future silently slips away;

In the days of my youth
I was much better than the rest,
painting my world in a brighter hue,
but now I take a different view;

Kings fall to pawns as I strategically move
my affection from square to square,
a timid approach to another's waiting room,
but will arrogance feel my presence there;

Brother can you tell me . . .
has my wallpaper faded
to awaken the sleeping alleyways
that haunt me from day to day,
or should I plan to look another way?

Brother can you tell me . . .
how many rooms lie vacant down this hall,
or is it mine and that is all,
the shadows surround and stare in awe
as marble posters begin to fall;

Going Places

The digital age is here my friend,
would you like to take a spin,
for once you choose to enter
you'll never return again,
but once you've missed your train
a future unpolished can only fade,
and you'll have to walk your journey
from place to place, and day to day;
The patrons arrive at the turnstiles,
checking photographs at the front door
of the simple pleasures they knew before,
faces younger today than they were yesterday,
eager to catch that future wave,
and maybe if you work just a little harder
-- just a little faster, you'll shine like the rest,
or maybe stay up the rest of the night,
got to get those circuits right,
or compete with the grand, new design,
make those deliveries right on time;
The restless data streams travel in wolf packs,
silent surround and from every direction attack,
and when your configuration is outdated
they overrun your feeble perimeter,
toss you into the scrap pile to retire
with the other pieces of obsolete hardware;
Such sacrifice when payment is due
should you awake to find yourself
old when the day is new,
witness the tulips' last bloom,
find colors once vibrant in the days of youth
begin to dull and fade from view;
The data streams strike day and night
as fresh recruits race their brand-new,
bored-out, computer terminals in blazing pursuit,
running off to faraway places that glimmer
in the distance, but not arriving in the end,
the digital age is here my friend.

A Slide Too High

As a child
I stood in line
excited to ride
the wild, water slide,
but as those days
fall behind
I dream of things
I'll never find:
A sonic dive
screaming by
the cascaded echoes
of a canyon sky;
It is the only thing
that can satisfy
my grown desire;
So instead I ride
the raging riptide
within the lust
of another's eyes,
or surf the psychedelic
pages of the mind
in search of places
that are real sometimes,
for no one builds
that high anymore,
the preschool, water slides
I once adored.

The Day Before

I took just a sip
deep with desire,
you were the match,
and I the forest fire;
Sultry emotions spin
into the runaway clouds
of a storming hurricane
that wouldn't last the day,
for even though
you wore the same face
you returned as another,
leaving me to ever wait
for the one I once adored,
-- the one who came the day before;

Moonbeams dance from shore to shore
for the one who came the day before;
Seagulls sing to sunset fiords
for the one who came the day before;
Serene skies calm unrelenting storms
for the one who came the day before;
Balcony, champagne memories pour
for the one who came the day before;

The interest once shared between only two
lingers solely within the selfless one;
Footstep whispers upon morning dew
fade to yesterdays on the run;
Still they keep me waiting
in shadows behind the sun,
for the one who came the day before,
-- the one who comes no more.

The Polish and Poise of Pretty Boys

Pretty boys hold pretty girls,
promising fancy pearls,
they leave them scattered -- forever lost,
in waters all around the world;

Pretty boys hold pretty boys,
filling their fountains with coins,
leaving them to ever search
for guarantees to fill the voids;

Whispers soothe those wanting lips
they learn to play so well,
still some ponder which wistful words
they might be willing to sell;

Hands slip behind the steering wheels
of smooth and silky limousines;
Serene, the waltz of heartbeat rhythms
that purr all along the midnight beach;

They glimmer in grandeur upon princely balconies,
fueled by the champagne of frenzied fantasies;
With vampire eyes they sweep the city streets,
seeking fresh, one-night lovers on which to feed;
Can there ever really be a single choice
for the polish and poise of pretty boys?

Daybreak awakens
to the rhythmic tease
of a man's, pale cologne
sailing out of reach.

Lost Planes . . .
Lost Planes Again

The planes that go down
inside my head,
sometimes I wish
I were there instead;
Gray clouds march
in a parade without rest
over colors blue,
over colors red,
over all other colors I once knew;
I search for something more to find,
but these things I'll leave behind;
If I boarded today
would it be too soon,
for the planes go down,
-- the planes go down again,
and this time I'm sure
the parade will end.

Wonderland Waltz

A diamond glimmers
not like the memory
of a wonderland waltz,
so elegant and free;

How far we wandered
the paths unpaved,
on our midnight journeys?

An island paradise for two
where delicate wishes,
and gentle kisses
caress the moonlight glow;

Your breath upon mine,
our passionate whispers
weave deep into the night;

Each moment an eternity
in our youth and vigor,
but time does not linger;

For mine are the windswept petals
of a waltz in wonderland;
I hold only the stem,
and wait for the buds
of a dream to bloom again.

Intimate Circles

Hands upon hers, upon his;
Hands upon his, upon hers;
Nothing can ever feel wrong,
when nothing can be sure,
one can never be enough
when we only hunger for more;
Emotions rise and waterfall inside,
as once again we begin to discern
the difference between boys and girls;
The wonder of the masterpiece
before the paint begins to dry,
and it matters not who nor why
for everything feels like wine tonight;

Once-upon-a-time
the choice was mine,
once-upon-a-time,
till the vampire smiled:
"I need the drug
that brings me lust,
I need the drug
so I can love;"

Tomorrow awakens today,
and I feel the crave
to replay every frame
in the yesterday that made
you glance my way,
but your footsteps pale . . .
your footsteps pale . . .
against the thunder
of the midnight rain.

The Days That Remain

Behind the windows
of a passing train,
I catch a glimpse
of your quiet pain;
Your scream is twin
to the friendless dog
whipped and beaten
for the want of love;
You thought for so long
this could never happen
to a man so big, so strong,
but I can hear your wide cry
reaching deep into the night
for a compassion warm
within the frost, covered puddles
where you dip your line;
The turpentine flows across
your dream ridden eyes,
and suddenly only tie-dye skies
recall the innocence of days gone by;
Yes, you thought for so long
this could never happen
to a man so big, so strong,
but now you realize
that you were wrong
as you stare behind
at the ravaged lawn,
thinking of other places
you might have gone.

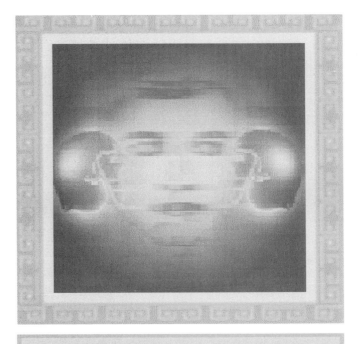

V. The Room of Youth

The Room of Youth

How many times we've tried to return across the shattered, stepping stones strewn all along those reckless lanes of youth? We ever reach for the vibrant images which only glanced in our rear-view mirrors when memory was short of breath. How we wish we could relive those times again: The times when we closed our eyes, using the roll of the dice to decide; the times when we followed our instincts, and gave into our passion. We failed to even slow as we approached those winding, high-speed lanes, finding rest in the five-minute parking zones scattered intermittently along the way. We were unaware of the countless days that passed, each setting sun stealing the final brushstrokes of masterpieces never to be seen by eyes again. Years seemed to pass before we came to realize, the pennies once tossed so carelessly away would only turn to gold someday.

Lipstick Tease

The islands burn bright,
transforming the Winter's night
into a private paradise
where young emotions run wild
beneath the neon lights;
Glamour girls polished
in painted nails and faces,
drive by in sleek automobiles
to flirt with the new boy of sixteen,
manning the pumps at the filling station;
Some slide into the warmth
of open bays in a seductive way,
past the row of parked cars
serviced earlier that day;
Rough engines run smooth,
and purr to the borrowed echoes
of second hand shop stereos
when he sends the vehicles away,
offering a humble wave
to tuned rear-view mirrors;
Lights that once burned bright
begin to drift and fade away,
joining the steady, scarlet stream
of tail lights racing along the highway;
A new customer
swaggers up to the island:
Tinted, power windows
move with the ease
of a stripper's tease,
revealing a subtle hint
of the driver's intent;
The attendant smiles
in his usual, casual style
then exhales silver, smoke rings
over the slippery memory
of some lovely, young girl
he knew only moments before.

A Passing Wave

Behind the taunting window
of the house next door,
the blinds are drawn
into a seductive pose;
In his thoughts he sees her,
hands softer than whispers
to brush away the splinters
embedded in his youth;
He ponders whether
she will ever
get to know him,
-- the boy next door . . .
for seasons change,
and it wouldn't be long

She smiles inside her bedroom,
breath gentle as Summer rain;
In a diary she becomes absorbed
with words written on the page;
In her thoughts she sees him,
eyes mild ripples in the lake
to wash away the insecurities
she tries to hide deep inside;
She ponders whether
he will ever
get to know her,
-- the girl next door . . .
for seasons change,
and it wouldn't be long

before the fingertips of Summer
touched the fingertips of Fall;

On the wave of a passing glance they are tossed between
the fringes of opportunity, and a fairy tale dream;
In their hearts they drive nimble, red, sports convertibles
naked to the wind, racing and increasing speed;

They wander far beyond the watercolor boundaries
of the playgrounds they knew in innocence,
churning passion into kaleidoscope adventures,
-- impulsive and ever-changing in the revolving light;

As mild Summer nights paint into a reflective glimmer,
Autumn looms over the horizon catching them unaware,
releasing the tide that leaves them ever searching
for traces of the sand castle paradise they left behind;

For how quickly the blooms of youth change in season
when masterpieces surrender to the glitter of poster imitation?
How many colors we failed to perceive except in passing memory,
after fingertips of Summer touched the fingertips of Fall?

Watercolor Rain

Snow falls upon its quiet rails
as the years begin to spin away,
and no one else recalls your name
except the one you led astray;
All lessons and principles
learned in an earlier day,
blurred by multicolor raindrops
racing down the side of a page;
You were more than twice my age
when the art gallery bathed
in the shade of watercolor rain;
Stained glass curtains opened
and never closed again;
I was the quiet stranger
when led by the sweat of my hand
to the rumbling waterfalls
of some faraway, foreign land;
The ready room at the top of the stairs
dimmed when no one else was there;
Every night we thundered down
those screaming, runway lanes,
leaving the evening haze of city lights
and our cloudy pasts behind;
Fleeting images fill those forbidden nights
that forever flicker within candlelit frames;
They hang upon the hidden hallways of my mind
safely tucked behind an occasional smile;
-- Do I pass before your glimmering eyes
every once in a while in days gone by,
for often I wonder where you are today,
and whether you even recall the name
of the high school boy of seventeen
left standing in the watercolor rain.

Midnight Runners

Midnight runners
race from stoplight to stoplight,
tires screaming from the pain
of being first to arrive;
Victory streamers and racing stripes
paint multicolor streaks across the night,
until lights rise from green to red,
and chrome-polished bumpers
stand even once again;
The night streams in
through rolled down windows
as I engage cruise control,
gliding at slow, steady speed
past the rusting ghosts
of abandoned Mustangs and GTOs:
Midnight runners with engines
that breathed fire and flame
in the days of their youth,
but raced ahead at such speed,
they lived and died
in the same world
in which they were born.

For Fear of Bridges

The heart can reach
a thousand miles further
than eyes can see
when the words
of faraway letters speak,
and faded images
of photographs breathe;
Sometimes I wonder
whether I should repeat
the trace of words
that once fell unheard,
for when looking back
on all of the bridges
I failed to cross,
I can only ponder
how much longer
before they crumble,
before they forever fall.

Final Photographs

Aged, final photographs stare
with the melancholy eyes
of an abandoned child
when treasured faces
which so proudly sailed
the earlier album pages
begin to fade and disappear;
We watched with such little regard
as the precious petals
within our own back yards
fell silent, wilted, and then died:
-- the friendships we thought
would never slip by . . .
And now how our sunsets fade
when the empty expressions
of hazed, back-window panes
gaze at scattered, marble remains,
and masterpieces left in the rain;
How many times we tried
to reach far behind
the rusted, barriors of time
for the pennies once paid,
on what we then thought
was just another passing day;
We can only sit
inside our shaded rooms,
deep and brooding blue,
in vivid detail recall the way
footsteps pale took center stage,
when we first composed
our movie-star smiles
with such glamour, such grace
for the final photographs
we would ever take.

Another James Dean

He was born
of those country cornfields
where conservative roots run deep,
and once he strongly embraced
conventional, country beliefs,
but as a teen it seemed
his collar had been caught
on the rungs of a whirlwind,
running and increasing speed,
and he would never break free,
for from that day forth
no one would ever know
from which direction
he would come,
or even when he would go;
The currents he would often seek
led to perilous extremes,
his head recklessly dipping
beneath the stormy waves,
still never a hand he would take,
for no experience he would forsake,
but his smile could chase away
the wind and rain of a hurricane,
sweep you into a Summer's day,
and make you forget the pain
if only for a single day
when he'd leave you once again
on his restless search for rainbow colors
he might never find,
just a careless wave good-bye,
and even the sun would wipe
the mist from her sullen eyes;

Some would claim
he'd venture into shadows
where wicked people go,
and sometimes even carried
evil in his soul,
but I can see those spinning tires
as he slides from side to side,
slipping on the ice of inexperience,
and skirting the rusting guardrails
strung along the twisted turns
of winding, high-speed curves;
He displays composed dexterity,
still I am haunted by the fear,
he may not live to see youth pass
in those racing, rear-view mirrors.

Endless Interlude

Suddenly swept into an 80's dance saloon
where the music seemed so fresh, so new,
extravagance maneuvered to win my view,
but within my eyes there was only you;

Dressed in our innocence and youth,
and weightless in our dancing shoes,
we waltzed in waves from room to room
every passing hour from dusk till noon;

The kaleidoscope churned and burned,
pursuing the colors inside my head,
-- passionate, candy apple reds,
or shady, autumn blues instead;

      -- Too much --
      -- Too fast --
      -- Too afraid --
      -- it wouldn't last --

      -- One night r-e-a-c-h-e-d --
      -- into the next --
      -- without taking --
      -- a single breath --

And every day I loved you true,
every day from July till June,
even when dawns failed to bloom,
and the weekends left too soon,
when monsoon winds raped and ruined,
our sapphire, seaside afternoons;

Let us play once again: "The Endless Interlude",
drowned within the wake of dusk till noon,
for just the hint of your pale perfume
can spin me back into that 80's dance saloon;

A Roll Away Kiss

You want her,
but your best friend
is such a charming, young man
who can dance with the best,
and with just a passing glance
he slips inside your humble embrace
to sweep the young girl's heart away,
loving the one you cannot have,
and leaving you with the lonely ones
who stand along the sidelines,
. . . the pages fly by . . .
. . . the pages fly by . . .
much faster than time can recall,
the pale fragrance of a love song
written but never played,
solemn words fall clumsy
at such a fresh and gentle age,
and although chocolate-covered lies
seem to hide well behind moonlit eyes
when whispered words caress,
and fall smooth past parted lips:
. . . the pages fly by . . .
. . . the pages fly by . . .
much faster than love can recall,
the bona fide promises made
on a night that was swept away
by dawn of the very next day.

A Pale Farewell

I wish today
I could paint the rain
that tiptoes upon
the scattered pages
of our college days;
End-over-end
the loose-leaf sheets
somersault into the wind,
never to be seen
by eyes again;
In silence I breathe
these journeys deep,
a desperate moment
before you turn to leave,
. . . r-e-a-c-h-i-n-g . . .
. . . r-e-a-c-h-i-n-g . . .
for those naive dreams
once green in the trees
that will forever only
toss and tumble helplessly
upon lonely, autumn streets;
My cruise ship now
begins to sink,
and it seems
everything will be
swallowed by the sea,
for the ocean is selfish,
filled with jealousy,
she surrenders nothing
except the
- - h - a - u - n - t - i - n - g - -

I wish today
I could paint the rain
to hide the linger
in the eyes that say:
*"I wish you didn't
have to leave"*,
you -- the last lifeboat
sailing away from me.

VI. The War Room

The War Room

Winter touches my face tonight as I march in cadence with history. The band plays the same song it has for years and years; only the names and the faces change. Once the military streets were paved, it seems there was little reason to change speed or even direction.

The clouds all along the horizon explode into a million dying faces. Below exhausted armies on endless search for something new to burn, but that is not my concern. In some distant memory life had a grace, but now how my heart, my eyes have paid. So difficult to focus on the near extremes when the space beyond - - - becomes the space b-e-t-w-e-e-n, and I ponder how long the deadbolts will hold when insanity thunders upon my door.

The memories of rented brotherhood are the stakes that pound into my beating heart. Young men, once proud and strong, bow to Medusa's eyes as human flesh and bone is transformed into an endless row of scattered headstones.

At battle's end, I listen to the wisdom of silence which rests upon the confused, puzzle pieces of a once grand, foreign city. As the smoke begins to clear, the first timid rays of sunlight touch my face the way mother used to. I cry for her as I lie in wait for death to bring me home.

Drowning in the Burn

Fire and flame -- the burning bridges,
filled my eyes as a child;
It is the smoke that clears,
but never the memory;

For today I shuddered in the trenches,
haunted by the endless tracers
which filled the nighttime sky,
claiming imaginary targets;

I have only flesh and skin to defend
against armor piercing thoughts and silence,
and distant you stand in the corners,
careful to avoid the ricochets;

I am wounded, and my spirit is laden
with the weight of the scars it carries,
still a weary, skeletal frame reaches
for you across the raging battlefield;

Won't you meet me outside the perimeter,
for love offers no protection
against the hidden mines
and barbed wire strands;

Won't you meet me outside the perimeter,
lest my breath slow to a whisper,
and entire existence
be remembered as nothing more.

The Rage of Retribution

Approaching the frenzied firestorm,
you search with ice cube eyes
for something more to burn
within the smoke that hides
the rubble of past paradise,
and the victims of fratricide;
. . . You feed the flames . . .
. . . You feed the flames . . .
with the bombs that fall,
consuming real and imagined
juggernauts in judgment halls;
-- Some call it an obsession,
the things you feel a need to prove,
but you can always choose
to only call it "payment due";
It bothers you not
in your grand facade
as you parade across
the frozen promenade,
all passing memories
of pain and pleasure
soon to be forever gone,
replaced by a napalm calm.

City Stalingrad (1942)

Frozen, bloody corpses
reinforce the city walls,
against the steady pounding
of artillery shells and bombs;

The smoke begins to thin
and drift in the wind
as two armies stand naked
ready to contend,
but advance suddenly halted
by haunting tranquillity,
the awed expressions -- disbelief,
reflected in eyes of humanity;

The ghost of the city,
-- a ghastly skeleton,
rises from the rubble
nearly in oblivion:

Nothing left to burn,
Nothing left to surrender,
Nothing left to defend,
Nothing left to remember;

Is this not Stalingrad,
so silent upon the pages of history,
so many branches burned and broken
within her family trees;

Is this not Stalingrad,
a deep and dismal landfill,
so much buried beneath the ruins,
so much remains there still.

Torpedo Squadron 8

So many empty lives
built up from your ashes,
the sound of your voices
silent in the past;
As I place my hands against the glass
I feel there is so much more,
but only photographs presented
in the display case memorial;
Countless vacant spaces
reside in family, photo albums,
adjacent to young faces
of men in naval uniforms;
You had wandered far from home,
skimming the wave tops,
your engines burning;
The radio broadcast
announced a great victory,
and that you were lost at sea,
but so many refused to believe;
For such was the hope
you would return that day
that even the sun lingered
in the sunset sky;
The years have passed,
but the men in the lookouts
still hear the hum
of your motors
lost out there somewhere
over the deep, Pacific ocean;
It's been years since and still I wait,
I can hear your motors running Torpedo 8,
won't you come home,
won't you please come home?

A Winter's Welcome

Confederate armies hold you hostage
to traditional values and ideologies,
and as long as your banners match theirs
there's no reason to question Gettysburg,
but the gold of Summertime never lasts
between those smoky, cannon blasts;
Brotherhood blooms, runs, then dies
right before one's melancholy eyes;
So one day I ran off on my own,
carried all sandbag titles that I must,
leaving naked, wire connections
that someday would only rust;
I tried to save my sanity,
but there was no getting away
from those bleeding, tar pit memories,
and the screams feeding those frenzied flames;

At the end of a bitter war
two . . .
three . . .
four years old,
ashen armies are returning home,
leaving me to face the winter alone;
For no country roads or outstretched arms
would ever welcome me home again;
No sympathetic eyes to greet mine,
my father, my brothers in time;
No stroke of a mother's touch
to soothe away the scrapes and cuts;
Day by dismal, dying day
I cry my tears of shame,
reaching for a hint
of forgiveness pale,
for I was only a child back then
traveling the wilderness lost,
who could not comprehend
what the sin would cost.

A Farewell to Reason

Two soldiers in a combat zone;
Two soldiers went in alone;
The bullets whip, the cannons groan;
Two soldiers not coming home;

Add years to this experience;
Knowledge breeds intelligence;
New ideologies, technologies,
super sonic speeds, NATO policies;

Two pilots in a combat zone;
Two pilots flew in alone;
Missiles flare, anti-aircraft groans;
Two pilots not coming home.

VII. The Inspiration Room

The Inspiration Room

Voices once forgotten reach from behind every passing corner when I wander along the backstreets of a place called home. The houses all seem familiar even as the names and the faces change. Bare trees now stand witness to the fields where I once played so free, while the bitter whispers of the winter wind passes through me.   But all along the cold and quiet road I am warmed by pleasant images of the past -- the gentle smiles of friends and family who may never come back. They will ever live comfortably within the plush hotels of memory.

A Monumental Toast

The faces behind the dusty windows
of my past will never disappear,
warm and friendly echoes
fill those winding hallways
of retrospection;
Yesterday's heroes stand fast
in the places they were left,
still their voices reach out to me
from behind every rugged crossroad
when suddenly I feel lost,
and unsure of which way to go;
To these this is truly dedicated,
may they ever be remembered
for the subtle ways each contributed
to the growth of just a simple man;
These humble gifts
I've learned to treasure,
for such a fine collection it is,
delicately selected
from personalized issues
of custom magazines;
-- The disparate clippings
fall like Autumn leaves,
through all the years of my life
they fall . . .
              they fall . . .
evolving the once empty page
into the living collage that is me.

Forever in a Day

Shy behind the smile
timid fingers of emotion
dreams away silent night,
-- sunrise kisses dawn;

Butterfly dances grace
upon the blooming
petals of a new day,
-- morning echoes fade;

Pale, seaward breeze once tossed
draws into a daydream waltz,
Solomon sings to shepherds lost,
-- two distant strangers called;

Crystalline glasses rise to wed,
honeymoon eyes meet instead;
Forever, amaretto afternoon
fills oceanside, hotel room;

The misty rays of another's touch
whispers warm upon wanting flesh,
lips meet lips in breathless rush,
-- seaside sky begins to blush;

"Good-night", candles' brewing glow;
"Good-night", incense and fading musk;
"Good-night", romantic one-day show;
"Good-night", -- sunset tucks in dusk.

Reunion for a Night

Last night didn't we seem to fly
far away from our day-to-day,
far away to places "once upon a time",
painted upon the preschool pages
of fairy tales and nursery rhymes;
We rode the wild and screaming highs
of winding, amusement park rides
once again for the very first time,
drinking in those pleasant yesterdays
we thought we'd left so far behind;
Didn't it feel good when we gathered
the coffee table cards once scattered,
recreating our past, poker-playing hands
of the conquests claimed years before,
debating who carried the winning score;
Was it you who danced the paper doll rings
formed by the hands of nightclub sororities?
One by one, we recalled the twilight names
of late-night ladies, who in our rooms remained:
"Yes, I still remember her well . . .
was it Lori, Susan, or Michelle?"
sometimes it was too difficult to tell,
and we might have never really known,
for those yesterdays . . . how they fell
row by racing, domino row,
still we tried to stitch the missing pieces
within our tapestries of tattered memories;
"Another shot!"
> \- - - to make it all too clear . . .

"Another shot!"
> \- - - to take us far from here . . .

far from the reign of late-night, working days,
far from the domesticated, "honey do" Saturdays,
far from the every day, pay-by-number routines,
far from the worries that haunt us when we sleep;

Let us ever savor the wine of treasured times,
and recall seasons past when time once smiled,
for memories . . . they sail with the sunset tide
where the cruise ships roam within our minds.

The Lamplighter

The wind whistles cold,
echoed by the tap dance
of lonely, stone pebbles,
and the shiver of glass;

The same wind whispers,
wrapping me
in the warmth of a smile,
the lamplighter arrives;

Time tumbles softly,
effortlessly like a drifting feather;
-- The lamplighter leaves,
time turns wicked again;

Mortality!
When will be the next?
When will be the last?
Each and every day
as a leper I wait;

For even in the darkest places
will the lamplighter appear,
as the face of a stranger,
or the face of a friend,
greeting today's journey,
or leaving once again.

Closing Words

Farewell . . .
           Farewell to reason
when all things end in season,
when nothing remains
except the memories imprisoned
in quiet, photograph frames;
Where have you been
my sunset friend,
what have you seen,
what have you felt,
for all recollections here
only seem to melt;
When I look across all the years
which took you from there to here,
I see the propellers of grandeur
turning . . .
           churning . . .
round, and round, and round,
but never really seeming
to ever leave the ground,
and now all I have
is the paper photograph
you left behind,
-- a pale moment
when you once smiled,
erasing the scars,
erasing the pain
of your history
that quietly remains;
It seems too inconsequential somehow
that your entire existence
is remembered only by the empty,
parking spaces left within the hearts
of those who knew you well.

Get extra copies of this book for your friends!!
Credit cards accepted!!

Call: 1-800-247-6553, or access web -- http://www.bookmasters.com.
When calling please provide the following information:

1) Name of Book -- A Farewell to Reason
2) Author -- Echo
3) Publisher -- Painted Petals Press

Pricing Information:

Qty	Price	Shipping	Total
1-2	$11.95 ea.	$4.00 ea	$15.95 ea
3-4	$11.95 ea	$3.00 ea	$14.95 ea
5-9	$9.95 ea	$2.50 ea	$12.45 ea
10+	$8.95 ea	$2.00 ea	$10.95 ea

ATTENTION COLLEGES, UNIVERSITIES, & CORPORATIONS:
Additional quantity discounts are available on this book.

Special Offer!! Obtain personalized, author signed copies of this book!! Just send send coupon below, and a check or money order in the amount of $20.00 (per book) payable to "Painted Petals Press".

Please send me ___ (how many?) personalized author signed copy (s) of: "A Farewell to Reason". Enclosed is a check or money order in the amount of $_____ payable to "Painted Petals Press".

Painted Petals Press
10151 University Blvd., Suite 316
Orlando, FL 32817